Illustrated and designed by
Arkadia Illustration
and Design.

Published by
Grandreams Limited
Jadwin House,
205/211 Kentish Town Road,
London, NW5 2JU.

Printed in Italy

CONTENTS

THE CEASELESS FIGHT TO SAFEGUARD EARTH

Common visions of Earth's future range from a bleak, grey,post-holocaust world full of near-starving and constantly-warring human survivors, to a cleaner, but still sinister, scenario where the brainwashed masses have everything they could wish for - except their individuality and freedom of thought.

But life in the 21st century is in fact a long way from either of these extremes. True, there are more gadgets to help make everyday life run more smoothly. Public transport has been upgraded beyond recognition (but still goes wrong from time to time) and normal people - as they do today - still work, get married, give birth and die. Crime, conflict and corruption still exist, but so do loyalty, love and selflessness. In short, things are not very different to the way we know them now; on the surface that is.

World peace remains a distant dream, as parts of the troubled former Soviet Union continue to be at constant war with their neighbours; but now the aggressors use relentless robot tanks instead of battalions of men. Deep beneath the surface of the globe's oceans exists another major threat, with Titan and his Aquaphibian followers constantly formulating new plans to undermine, and eventually extinguish, the human race.

In an attempt to democratically solve many of man's problems, the World Government has been established and that in turn has engineered the creation of an international security super-force, Spectrum. Just as white light spans the complete range of colours, so Spectrum covers the entire range of world security, with full police powers both on earth and in space. Operating 24 hours a day from Cloudbase - its seven-mile-high, free-floating headquarters - Spectrum's task of keeping the peace proves to be well within its capabilities.

However, in the year 2065, Spectrum's brief reign is suddenly and irreversibly altered by the Mysterons; an intangible and hostile alien race which soon proves to be the most deadly threat humankind has ever had to face.

Had Spectrum not been in place, it seems likely that the Mysterons would swiftly have succeeded in their ultimate aim: the systematic and complete destruction of the earth.

Fortunately for the human race, the combination of Spectrum's hand-picked core team all brave and brilliant in their various fields of expertise - with its fleet of the world's most advanced land and air vehicles, gives the organisation the power to fend off each Mysteron threat, safeguarding the world against destruction.

This time , however, the battle is more than tough. Seeking vengeance for what they mistakenly believed was an attack on their Martian base, the Mysterons prove ruthless, relentless and often cryptic opponents and all of Spectrum's highly-trained 600 personnel have come to dread their unearthly monotone messages of doom, more often than not beginning with the words " This is the voice of the Mysterons. Our next..." Not only are the Mysterons unseen, they are also all-seeing. As well as deliberately killing key human targets in order to create duplicates who will carry out their evil plot, they are also able to spot the accidental deaths that unfortunately still occur all too frequently on Earth, seizing on these as further opportunities to wreak havoc on humanity.

The Mysterons' formidable ability to duplicate does not stop at human beings. They are able to copy the molecular structure of anything, from animated life forms to inanimate objects. When the Mysterons threaten to destroy the City of London, for example, the driver of a truck transporting a sensitive nuclear device through the capital watches in helpless horror as his vehicle's controls mysteriously take on a life of their own. On another occasion, the Mysterons destroy a communications satellite, enabling them to replicate not only the shell of the vessel, but all of its complex computerised internal workings as well as an entire human crew.

At first glance, it seems this awesome power will undoubtedly secure victory for the Mysterons. But even aliens make mistakes and it is, ironically, one of their rare mistakes that turns what should have been their greatest asset into their biggest obstacle: Captain Scarlet™ himself.

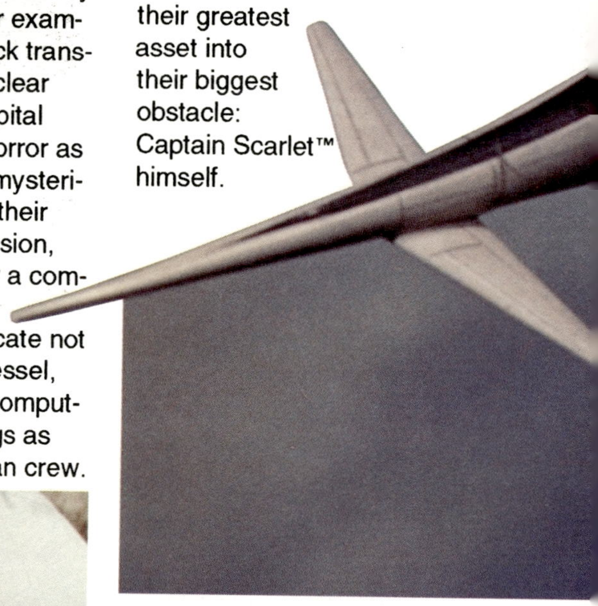

The Mysterons kill the original Captain Scarlet as he and Captain Brown rush to the rescue of the World President. As the life rapidly ebbs from his body, the Mysterons create an exact duplicate. Their oversight in the case of Scarlet was that as well as copying the molecular structure of his body, they also copied his brain patterns. These lay dormant in the body of the replica until the Mysterons had no further use for it, at which point the original brain reasserted itself. Thus the Mysterons have given Spectrum a piece of the unique power they wanted to reserve exclusively for themselves: indestructibility combined with living intelligence.

The crowning glory of Spectrum's tight team stationed at Cloudbase, Captain Scarlet proves again and again that he is more than a match for his opposite num-

ber, Mysteron Agent Captain Black. Not only can Scarlet rapidly regenerate his damaged body time and again after being pronounced "dead', he is also invaluable to Spectrum as a Mysteron early warning device, being able to sense their radiation field.

But however resilient and resourceful Captain Scarlet might be, he is still only one man. And in spite of the brilliance of his closest colleagues Colonel White, Captain Blue, Lieutenant Green and Spectrum's Interceptor pilots, the Angels, they represent an organisation with human limitations.

For everyone at Spectrum, as well as their agents across the globe, life is lived on the edge, never knowing when or from where the next Mysteron threat will come. Cloudbase may possess the most advanced technology known to man, but it cannot see its alien enemies, let alone predict their next move. Nor can it see into the future, which, if the Mysterons have their way, could perhaps be a blessing.

QUIZ!

Find out how much you really know about Spectrum and its arch-enemies, the Mysterons, in this twenty-question quiz. The first three questions appear below, the rest are distributed throughout the annual, so make sure you don't miss any. You'll find the answers on page 45 - but no cheating!

1. How many personnel has Cloudbase?

2. Who gives the order which ultimately causes the Mysterons to mount their attack on Earth?

3. What aquatic hobbies does Captain Blue enjoy?

WHITE AS SNOW

The satellite seemed to hang suspended, reflecting the stars; a tiny metal speck in the black,infinite wastes of space.

Inside, Bob Leck spoke into his mike, pop music playing in the background:

"I'll have that service report ready after transmission, Control."

"Right you are, TVR 17 - after all, we wouldn't want to interrupt the late show", replied the Controller.

"Don't tell me you've got time to listen to it!" joked Bob.

"Well, you know how it is Bob - it can get pretty dull down here on Earth compared to the life you space jockeys lead!" the Controller laughed back.

After confirming TVR 17's schedule for re-entry into the Earth's atmosphere for 14.00 hrs the next day, the Controller switched off his mike and leant back in his chair, ready to relax into the long, quiet night shift ahead. Hearing a slight noise from the door, he wheeled around to see a tall, sinister figure with a pallid face and cold, piercing eyes pointing a gun at him.

"W-Who are you?"

At the control of TVR 17, Bob was prepared to transmit his service report.

"Ok, Control. That report's ready for you now."

The speakers remained silent, as Bob repeatedly tried to raise a response from Earth, to no avail.

Inside the Control Tower, Bob's counterpart sat bound and gagged, hearing with mounting dread the futile attempts to contact him and watching helplessly as Captain Black took over the instruments. Black found the lever he was looking for, and as he pushed it down, Bob's voice came over the speakers again, this time with sharp alarm:

"What are you doing, Control? We're losing altitude. We...we're heading for re-entry! We'll burn up!"

As the incongruous music reached a crescendo, TVR 17, its man made shell pushed beyond endurance, exploded in a huge ball of flame, leaving only blackened, smoking fragments to spiral down in the cold, still air.

Life was over for Bob and the rest of the satellite's twelve-strong crew. But back in space, at precisely the spot where TVR 17 should have been, another craft had appeared. Identical down to every nut, bolt and carbon copy of Bob and his crew members, the Mysteronised satellite continued on its orbital path, playing the same music Bob had heard as he drew his last breath.

4. How is Captain Scarlet able to detect a Mysteron before anyone else?

5. What process commonly used in hospitals proves invaluable in exposing Mysterons?

6. What is the only surefire way of killing a Mysteron?

The atmosphere on Cloudbase's Control Deck was unusually relaxed. The world's top communications wizard, Lieutenant Green, sat dreamily tapping his foot to the music that played over the speakers, while Spectrum's most valuable Agent, Captain Scarlet,™ lounged with red -booted feet up on his Commander In Chief's Control Console.

"This is supposed to be an operational base, not a rest centre!" barked Colonel White, entering the Control room. As Scarlet and Green hastily tried to cover their embarrassment, he went on to mutter, "Well, I suppose it's harmless enough", adding that in spite of the remarkably clear reception, the music should be turned down.

"I can't, Sir!" said Lieutenant Green, as the music got louder and louder; "It's jammed!"

Throughout Cloudbase, off duty personnel winced, covering their ears with their hands, as Lieutenant Green checked his control panel for the source of the fault.

"Colonel White!", he exclaimed, "I've picked up something on the radar. It's the satellite TVR 17, Sir. Range 87 miles. Speed...mach 3.2. And the course...Collision course!"

"OUR NEXT ACT OF RETALIATION WILL BE TO KILL THE COMMANDER IN CHIEF OF SPECTRUM, COLONEL WHITE."

As Lieutenant Green monitored the satellite's rapidly-diminishing impact time, the Colonel's finely-tuned military instincts sprang into action.

"Captain Scarlet, launch Angel One. Orders - seek and destroy".

"No!, replied Scarlet, to Lieutenant Green's amazement.

"I gave an order, Captain." Colonel White's tone was icy and did not allow for further dispute.

"Yes, Sir", muttered Scarlet, glowering mutinously at his superior as he thought with horror of the dozen crew aboard the satellite.

"S.I.G!", sang back Symphony Angel, shooting sky wards with a roar to meet the fast approaching satellite. Visual contact was made almost immediately and, timing it to the last fraction of a second before impact, the Interceptor fired. As TVR 17 burst into flames for the second time, Angel One reported back to Cloudbase: "Direct hit. Total destruct. I repeat, total destruct."

At Cloudbase, Captain Scarlet™ was still wrestling with his anger over Colonel White's seemingly heartless order to destroy the satellite, when the call came for the Captains to assemble in the Control Room. Minutes later, Colonel White explained what he proposed to do:

7. On discovering the answer to question 6, which weapon did Spectrum create?

8. What was Captain Scarlet's special distinction in the World Army Air Force before he joined Spectrum?

"In view of the Mysteron's latest threat, I intend to leave immediately for a secret destination. Captain Scarlet, I would like you to take control in my absence."

"Is that an order, Sir?" asked Scarlet tonelessly.

"No, a request", replied the Colonel.

"Then I'm afraid I must decline."

"I see", remarked the Colonel, seemingly unruffled: "Captain Blue?"

"It would be an honour, Sir", replied Blue, bristling with pride.

As Colonel White left the Control room, Scarlet could not resist remarking again on what he believed to be a bad decision.

"You're wrong Captain",said Lieutenant Green quietly, "We received a report. The wreckage of the original TVR 17 was found three hours before the Mysteron replica attacked Cloudbase."

Shocked and more than a little ashamed, Scarlet exclaimed: "But why didn't he say anything? Does anyone know where he's gone?"

"I know", replied Green, "But I have my orders. I'm saying nothing."

Over the flat steely grey of the ocean, a helicopter whirred; the only sign of life in the foreboding sky. Its white-haired passenger, dressed simply in a fisherman's knitted sweater and hat, ordered the pilot to take her down.

"Here? But we're fifty miles from land! Are you gonna swim home?"

The passenger simply repeated the order with quiet insistence and the astonished pilot complied. As they hovered lower, the sea's inscrutable surface began to boil and bubble and within seconds the darkly gleaming deck of a submarine had risen out of the water.

"Wow!", exclaimed the pilot,"Are you some big shot in the Navy?"

"No", replied the disguised Colonel White, "I'm a deep sea fisherman."

Once he was safely winched down onto the deck, the submarine's Captain welcomed him aboard, introducing him to the crew as Robert Snow. Motioning the Colonel below, the Captain gave the order to clear the deck and take her down to ten fathoms.

Preparing to follow his crew members below deck, Seaman Soames, sent off balance by a freak wave, slipped and caught his foot in a loose chain. Cursing, he tried to free himself, exasperation turning swiftly to panic as he realised what was happening. As the water rose, he beat frantically on the ungiving metal door. It was too late. Within seconds the sea had recovered its indifferent calm and the only sign left of the sub's existence was the body of Soames, floating lifeless on the surface.

On the sub's bridge, the Captain ordered one of his men to act as Mr. Snow's steward and to show him to his quarters.

"Yes Sir", replied Soames, and with an undertone of ironic menace added, "I will take care of Mr. Snow."

At Cloudbase, Captain Blue was making the most of his temporary power. After ordering the three on-duty Angels on yet another round of target practice, he instructed a resigned-looking Lieutenant Green to assemble all off-duty personnel in the sick bay, where he had arranged a lecture.

"They're not going to like it Captain", sighed Green, "But you're in charge."

In the Amber Room, Lieutenant Green's voice interrupted the relaxed atmosphere: "...assemble in the sick bay, where Doctor Fawn will give you a lecture on the physiology of the lower primate."

"A talk on monkeys! That's all we need!" exclaimed Rhapsody Angel. Her companions agreed, echoing her plea for the rapid return of Colonel White.

In the cavernous metallic labyrinth of the submarine's lower deck, light footsteps slowly approached 'Snow's' cabin. Gun at the ready, Soames stealthily tried the handle and silently pushed open to see 'Snow's' back turned to him.

"We will be avenged, Colonel White", proclaimed Soames, in a flat, deadly tone, raising his gun as he savoured the approaching victory for the Mysterons. But faster than a striking snake, the chair whipped around, its occupant firing a shot which narrowly missed Soames, puncturing a pipe and filling the room with steam.

"What's going on down there !" demanded the Captain, as the alarm sounded on the bridge.

"Someone's sealed off the bulkhead, Sir, and I heard shots!"

9. What does Colonel White believe to be Captain Scarlet's only failing?

The Captain and his two right-hand men swiftly went into action, and, reaching the scene in seconds, began to work on the sealed metal door with a blow-torch. Progress seemed agonisingly slow, as their sense of urgency increased tenfold at the sound of more shots.

On the other side of the door, the Mysteronised Soames had his prey cornered.

"You've got no chance, Earthman. I'm coming in."

Soames' shot caught his opponent full in the chest and, as he fell to the floor, his dying fingers gripped the trigger in a final, desperate gesture; his last bullet finding, and silencing, its gloating Mysteron target.

Seconds later, the dismayed Captain and his men surveyed the scene of battle, complete with two lifeless bodies.

"I don't understand!" exclaimed the Captain, "I want this ship searched with a fine tooth comb. Snow MUST be found!"

At that moment, muffled shouts came from the direction of the cabin's locker. In two strides, the Captain wrenched open the door, to reveal a bound and gagged, extremely flustered, but very much alive Colonel White!

The Captain gaped in disbelief, from the man in the locker to the man on the floor.

The minute the gag went off: "I knew it!" bellowed Colonel White, "I'll have your commission for this, Scarlet!"

As the Colonel continued to bluster furiously, the Captain and his men looked from one to another awkwardly.

"You don't seem to appreciate, Sir. This man is dead."

"That's no excuse!" snapped Colonel White.

Back at Cloudbase and on form, Colonel White barked out orders.

"Lieutenant Green, get me those reports. And get me Spectrum HQ London..."

Hearing his familiar voice ordering them on target practice, the Angels smiled happily. Even in this mood, their Commander in Chief was preferable to Captain Blue and his reign of terror!

"...And WHERE is Captain Scarlet™?"

"Why Sir", said Lieutenant Green surprised, "He's been waiting outside for over an hour."

"Well get him in here then!"

As Scarlet approached the console, the Colonel's face was as unyielding as granite. Launching into a list of Scarlet's various misdemeanours - including impersonating a superior officer - his voice rose with his temper and culminated in:

"...You leave me no alternative. I sentence you to death."

Captain Scarlet's words broke the shocked silence that followed:

"I understand, Sir."

"But", continued the Colonel, "Since you are indestructible, I see little point in standing you up before a firing squad. Dismissed...And you can wipe that grin off your face, Lieutenant Green."

Once again surprised but delighted at his Commander's very British sense of humour, Green's reply was more than usually enthusiastic:

"Yes Sir, Colonel Sir!"

CROSSWORD

To test how well you know Spectrum see if you can complete the crossword below :

ACROSS

1. What must the Angels do before an enemy attacks Cloudbase?

2. Name an Angel pilot?

3. In 'White as Snow' where does Colonel White hide?

4. What can Captain Scarlet™ sense from the Mysterons?

5. What colour is at the centre of the Spectrum logo?

6. Name another Angel pilot?

7. Name someone else who flies with 2 and 6 across?

8. What do Spectrum personnel say when they are given an order?

9. What is the name of the pilots who protect Cloudbase?

DOWN

1. What did the Mysterons make Captain Scarlet?

2. What is Spectrum always ready for?

3. Who is in charge of communication at Cloudbase?

4, 5 & 6. What did Colonel White tell the Helicopter pilot in 'White as Snow' he did for a living?

7. Where do the Mysterons come from?

INDESTRUCTIBLE but not INHUMAN

Even in his previous life as Paul Metcalfe, Captain Scarlet™ cut an impressive figure. As the youngest colonel ever in the world Army Air Force, he was a crack pilot and weapons expert, at the peak of physical fitness. On top of this, his mental strength, a keen intelligence, sense of humour and compassion for others, made him a prime candidate for Spectrum.

By now the incredible story of Scarlet's transformation from mere mortal to indestructible super-hero is history; his courage, loyalty and indomitable spirit proved beyond doubt in countless successful missions.

But in spite of his unique qualities, Captain Scarlet remains as essentially human as Captain Blue, Lieutenant Green or any other member of Spectrum (and perhaps more so than his inscrutable Commander in Chief, Colonel White!)

For example, being indestructible does not mean being impervious to sensation. Captain Scarlet™ feels every blow and bullet he is subjected to, making his bravery - putting himself in physical danger time and again - even more outstanding.

During one Mysteron attack, Scarlet and Blue realise there is no other way to stop a speeding jet than by ramming it with the SPV. Blue - ever the realist - exclaims this would be suicide. Scarlet, even though he has only just been told of his indestructibility by Dr Fawn and not yet put to the test, ejects his friend to safety and puts his own life in peril.

On another occasion, Captain Scarlet exposes himself to 1000,000 volts worth of a force known to kill Mysterons: electricity, without knowing what effect it will have on him, but surely speculating that since he has been Mysteronised it could prove lethal.

OK, so - even with the pain factor - knowing you're indestructible must be a fairly big comfort when going into a potentially fatal situation. But who knows what indestructibility really means? For example, if Scarlet's body were to be blasted by a nuclear explosion into billions of fragments too small for the naked eye to see, would it really regenerate itself? Captain Scarlet and the Spectrum team simply do not know. Scarlet therefore, continues to lay down his life and suffer the extremes of pain for his colleagues and ultimately, his planet.

There is another aspect to Captain Scarlet's make-up that cannot be overlooked - even though Colonel White believes it to be his only fault: his impetuous nature. It would not be out of character, for instance, for Scarlet to openly disagree with the decisions of his superior; even, on more than one occasion, refusing an order outright. But stubborn pride is not a fault of Spectrum's top agent and he is always quick to apologise and make amends if found to be in the wrong.

Whatever the situation, we should not dismiss this side of Captain Scarlet, for perhaps it is this very human trait which enabled him to undergo Mysteronisation and live to tell the tale: as a free-thinking human being and not simply the soulless puppet of an enemy race.

On the page opposite are some scenes from Captain Scarlet's adventures, but the Mysterons have stolen the colour, see if you can put it back.

10. Where is the World Government based?

11. Which very human trait has Captain Black been known to display?

12. What makes Captain Scarlet's bravery so remarkable, in spite of his special powers?

MYSTERON or MOUSE

The seemingly limitless power of the Mysterons - with their ability to duplicate and control man, machine or beast - is by now well-known. The Mysterons may not be human, but who is to say they do not possess human - or even inhuman - weaknesses? Undertaking careful analysis of all the Mysteron 'incidents' to date, and piecing together (at times seemingly useless) fragments of information, Colonel White and his team are able to gain invaluable insights into what makes their enemies tick.

When the Mysterons attempt to assassinate General Tiempo, Commander of the Western Region World Defence, their Agent posing as a surgeon is discovered when he makes the mistake of exposing his hand on an X-ray film. Unlike the familiar monochrome negative image that would result in the case of a human, Spectrum discovers that with Mysterons a full positive image is the result - just as in a fully developed photograph.

This tiny chink in the Mysterons' armour enables Spectrum to develop the Mysteron Detector which, based on the X-ray process, proves of great help in exposing Mysterons.

In the same Mysteron attack, Captain Blue discovers that another force common on earth is also fatal to Mysterons: electricity. This leads to the creation of a new weapon - the Anti Mysteron Electron Gun. Even though bullets and conventional weapons may seem to kill Mysterons, appearances can be deceptive, and in fact the 'death' of the agent in these cases is the result of the Mysteron controllers simply shutting off the Agent's control signal due to failure of the mission.

The Electron Gun, however, performs two important functions which together prove fatal to Mysteron Agents. Firstly, it 'kills' the physical body of the Mysteron - electricity causes damage just as it would in a human. And secondly, it then blocks the Mysteron control signal from gettingthrough to the agent, preventing regeneration of the body.

Another Mysteron weakness lies in their inability to distinguish between dead or simply stunned human beings. When they attempt to destroy Futura City by killing and duplicating a leading World Air Force test pilot, Major Gravener, they make a big mistake in assuming the Major to be dead when he is in fact temporarily comatose.

Perhaps the most damaging weakness of the Mysteron controllers is one which Spectrum cannot be sure is general amongst Mysterons or specific only to Captain Black. This 'weakness' is one which recognise both as a strength and a universally human quality: compassion.

During a Mysteron attack, Black forces Symphony Angel into a radiation chamber, although he apologises to her, reassuring her that death will be swift. But in the event, he is unable to carry out this diabolical act and turns off the controls, with the words "Mysterons also have compassion."

So it seems the Mysterons have finer feelings too. Or could it be that this is just another example of their inhuman deviousness to convince Spectrum they are not invincible and to lull them into a false sense of security? Why, for example, should they show compassion for a human, when they show so little regard for their own agents on failing their missions? These questions give Colonel White and his crew endless potential problems to ponder over.

"AGENTS WE HAVE A PROBLEM !"

The Mysterons have captured some Spectrum agents, your task is to find them hidden in the wordsearch below:

Captains:
Scarlet
Grey
Magenta
Ochre
Blue
Green
White

Angels:
Destiny
Symphony
Harmony
Rhapsody
Melody

O J O W H I T E W E R T D C Y T
P O T N S C A R L D H M J Y R E R
E S T I N O M S C A H L E T U Y T R F G H
O A D R O F Y S C A L E T A O S E Y U H G R E S
T P B L U E P Y J G R E Y P C T R K I U U Y T R F
O K O T L O O M O E T P R S H I E N H T R E D E
L O O A P E R P T N R L O O R N D U Y T R N K J
H A R M O N Y H O T O E T D E Y O T R F D E W
P L E A S O F O K A G A E Y P E N H G R T R
O M E L O D Y N N O L S L O N H G T R
T O G R E E N Y S E O E K J H
E A T A W A S T R U B G F
R O S T A I N O M J U

SPV
SPV

SPOT THE DIFFERENCE

TREBLE CROSS
TWO MEN, IN WORLD AIR FORCE UNIFORM, DRIVE ALONG THE MOONLIT ROAD...
SLATON 15 MILES
A FEW MILES AHEAD, CAPTAIN BLACK MOVES ONTO THE ROAD IN AN UNMARKED TRUCK...
AS THE CAR RADIO PLAYS SOFT MUSIC, THE FAIR-HAIRED PASSENGER DOZES...
SPEEDING TOWARDS THEM IN THE OPPOSITE DIRECTION, CAPTAIN BLACK TURNS ON HIS EXTRA SET OF HEADLIGHTS...
CAUSING PANIC IN THE ONCOMING CAR...
LOOK OUT HARRIS!

IT IS TOO LATE...
INSCRUTABLE AS EVER, BLACK LOOKS ON AS THE BODY OF THE FAIR-HAIRED MAN FLOATS TO THE SURFACE..
...AND THEN TURNS TO HIS NEW COMPANION, A PERFECT REPLICA...
WE WILL DESTROY THE WORLD CAPITAL FUTURA CITY
MINUTES LATER, ANOTHER CAR APPROACHES THE SCENE...
LOOKS LIKE SOMEONE WENT OFF THE ROAD.
WE MAY BE ABLE TO HELP.
THE BODY FLOATS IN THE SAME PLACE...
LOOK! THERE IN THE WATER.
LETS GET DOWN THERE!

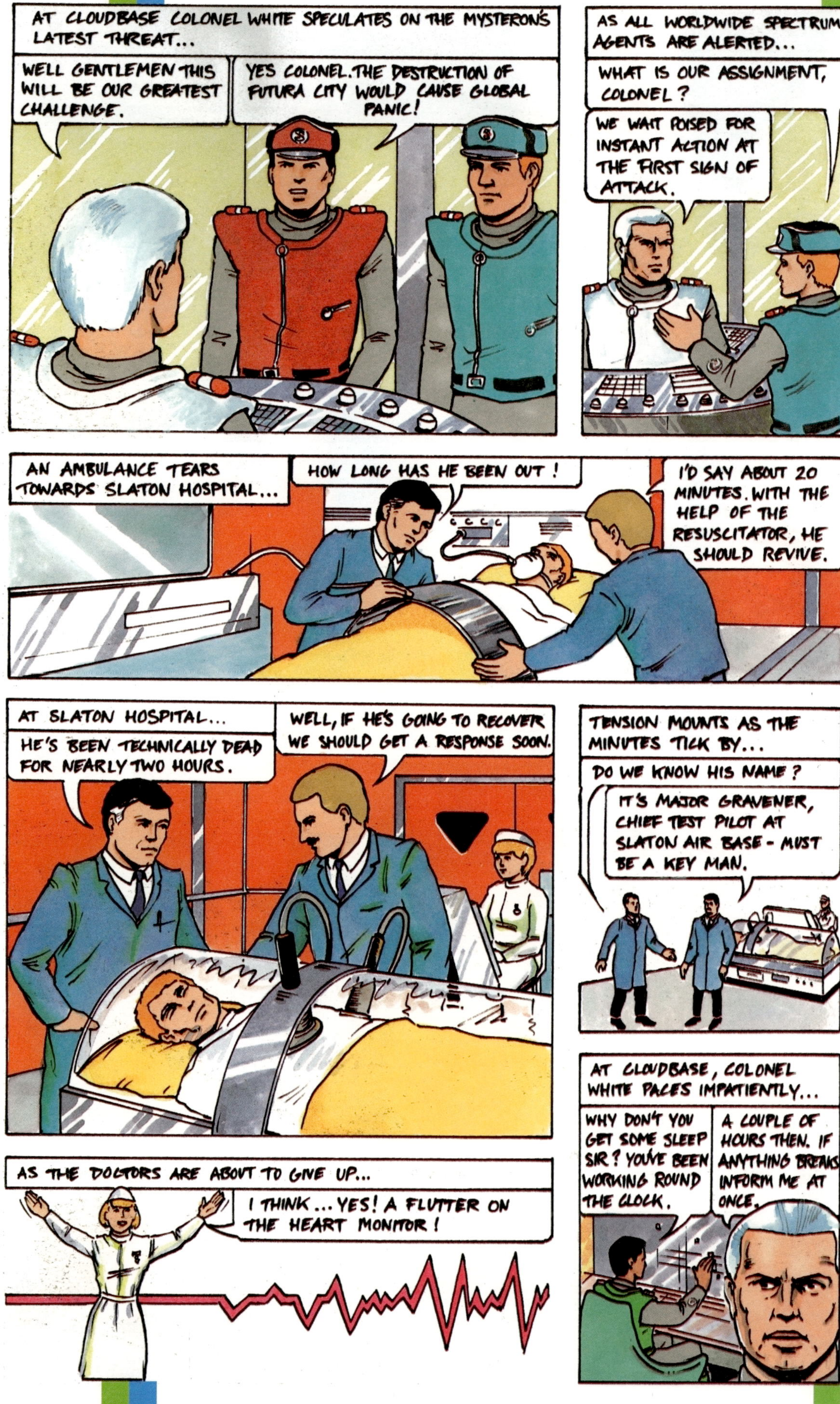
AT CLOUDBASE COLONEL WHITE SPECULATES ON THE MYSTERON'S LATEST THREAT...
WELL GENTLEMEN THIS WILL BE OUR GREATEST CHALLENGE.
YES COLONEL. THE DESTRUCTION OF FUTURA CITY WOULD CAUSE GLOBAL PANIC!
AS ALL WORLDWIDE SPECTRUM AGENTS ARE ALERTED...
WHAT IS OUR ASSIGNMENT, COLONEL?
WE WAIT POISED FOR INSTANT ACTION AT THE FIRST SIGN OF ATTACK.
AN AMBULANCE TEARS TOWARDS SLATON HOSPITAL...
HOW LONG HAS HE BEEN OUT!
I'D SAY ABOUT 20 MINUTES. WITH THE HELP OF THE RESUSCITATOR, HE SHOULD REVIVE.
AT SLATON HOSPITAL...
HE'S BEEN TECHNICALLY DEAD FOR NEARLY TWO HOURS.
WELL, IF HE'S GOING TO RECOVER WE SHOULD GET A RESPONSE SOON.
TENSION MOUNTS AS THE MINUTES TICK BY...
DO WE KNOW HIS NAME?
IT'S MAJOR GRAVENER, CHIEF TEST PILOT AT SLATON AIR BASE - MUST BE A KEY MAN.
AS THE DOCTORS ARE ABOUT TO GIVE UP...
I THINK... YES! A FLUTTER ON THE HEART MONITOR!
AT CLOUDBASE, COLONEL WHITE PACES IMPATIENTLY...
WHY DON'T YOU GET SOME SLEEP SIR? YOU'VE BEEN WORKING ROUND THE CLOCK.
A COUPLE OF HOURS THEN. IF ANYTHING BREAKS INFORM ME AT ONCE.

NEXT MORNING AT SLATON HOSPITAL...
WHERE AM I...? WHAT DAY IS IT...?
IT'S 9.17 AM, TUESDAY JULY 10TH. GET SOME REST NOW, WE'LL TALK AFTER LUNCH.
AT NEARBY SLATON AIR BASE A FAMILIAR FIGURE WATCHES COVERTLY...
INSIDE, THE DUTY OFFICER GREETS THE MORNING'S LATEST ARRIVAL...
GOOD MORNING MAJOR.
MAJOR GRAVENER WASTES NO TIME...
I WANT AN XK107 READY FOR TAKE OFF IN ONE HOUR, ARMED WITH A NUCLEAR WARHEAD.
A LIVE WARHEAD SIR?!
AMAZED BUT OBEDIENT, THE OFFICER PASSES ON THE ORDER TO CENTRAL CONTROL...
YES THAT'S WHAT HE SAID... I'LL GIVE YOU A WRITTEN ORDER TIMED AT 9.17 JULY 10TH
ONE HOUR LATER, THE XK107 IS READY FOR TAKE OFF...
THIS IS CAPTAIN BLACK RELAYING ORDERS FROM THE MYSTERONS. YOU KNOW WHAT TO DO...
BACK INSIDE THE BASE...
MAJOR GRAVENER...? AT THE HOSPITAL? BUT... YES GENERAL, WE'LL STOP HIM!

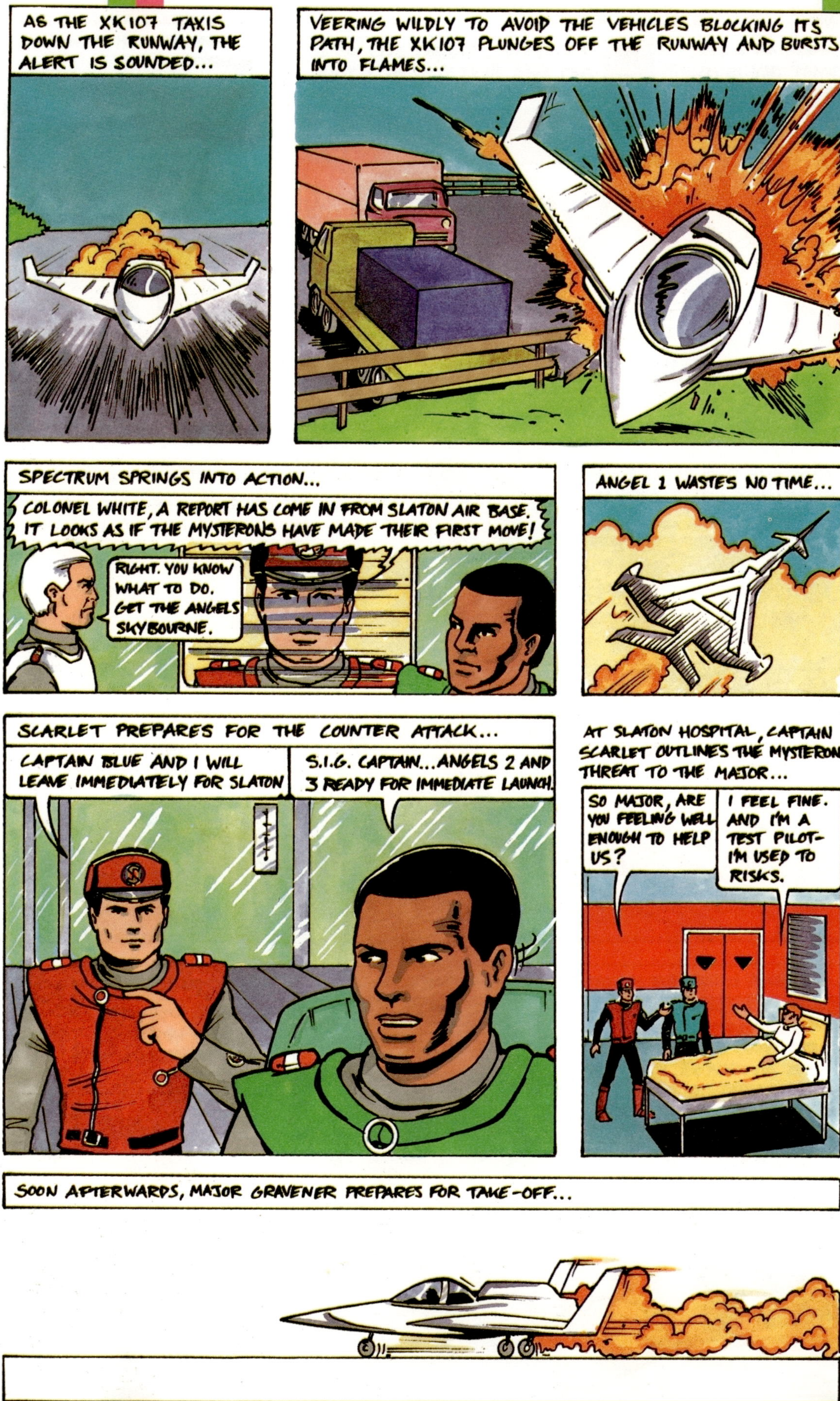

AS THE XK107 TAXIS DOWN THE RUNWAY, THE ALERT IS SOUNDED...
VEERING WILDLY TO AVOID THE VEHICLES BLOCKING ITS PATH, THE XK107 PLUNGES OFF THE RUNWAY AND BURSTS INTO FLAMES...
SPECTRUM SPRINGS INTO ACTION...
COLONEL WHITE, A REPORT HAS COME IN FROM SLATON AIR BASE. IT LOOKS AS IF THE MYSTERONS HAVE MADE THEIR FIRST MOVE!
RIGHT. YOU KNOW WHAT TO DO. GET THE ANGELS SKYBOURNE.
ANGEL 1 WASTES NO TIME...
SCARLET PREPARES FOR THE COUNTER ATTACK...
CAPTAIN BLUE AND I WILL LEAVE IMMEDIATELY FOR SLATON
S.I.G. CAPTAIN...ANGELS 2 AND 3 READY FOR IMMEDIATE LAUNCH.
AT SLATON HOSPITAL, CAPTAIN SCARLET OUTLINES THE MYSTERON THREAT TO THE MAJOR...
SO MAJOR, ARE YOU FEELING WELL ENOUGH TO HELP US?
I FEEL FINE. AND I'M A TEST PILOT-I'M USED TO RISKS.
SOON AFTERWARDS, MAJOR GRAVENER PREPARES FOR TAKE-OFF...

NEARBY, CAPTAINS SCARLET AND BLUE WATCH AND WAIT...
READY FOR TAKE-OFF CAPTAIN
RIGHT MAJOR WE'LL MAINTAIN DIRECT CONTACT ON THIS WAVELENGTH.
LETS HOPE WE CAN DECIEVE THE MYSTERONS BY REPLACING THEIR AGENT WITH THE REAL MAJOR...
... IN THE HOPE THEY'LL TELL HIM THE DETAILS OF THEIR PLAN TO ATTACK FUTURA.
LIEUTENANT GREEN KEEPS THE COLONEL POSTED...
THE MAJOR HAS BEEN AIRBOURNE 28 MINUTES. ANGELS AND SPECTRUM VEHICLES ARE IN POSITION ALONG HIS ROUTE.
SUDDENLY THE MAJOR'S HEADSET CRACKLES INTO LIFE...
THIS IS CAPTAIN BLACK RELAYING INSTRUCTIONS FROM THE MYSTERONS. YOU WILL LAND AT WESTON AIR STRIP...
CAPTAINS SCARLET AND BLUE LISTEN IN...
... I WILL BE WAITING.
THE SPECTRUM SALOON CAR SPEEDS TOWARDS IT'S DESTINATION...
WHERE IS WESTON AIRSTRIP?
ABOUT 30 MILES OUTSIDE FUTURA CITY LIMITS. IT HASN'T BEEN USED FOR YEARS.
AT THE ABANDONED AIRSTRIP, A FAMILIAR UNMARKED TRUCK LURKS IN THE EMPTY HANGAR...

THE ANGELS SOAR TOWARDS WESTON IN TIGHT FORMATION...
DESTINY ANGEL REPORTS BACK TO CLOUDBASE...
ARE YOU IN CONTACT WITH THE MAJOR?
YES, COLONEL. RANGE 27 MILES.
MAJOR GRAVENER STEALS HIMSELF FOR CONFLICT AS HIS DESTINATION LOOMS NEARER...
FAR BELOW ON TERRA FIRMA...
I THINK I SEE THE PLOT... TO TAKE THE NUCLEAR DEVICE TO WESTON, UNLOAD IT ONTO SOME OTHER VEHICLE, THEN USE THE XK107 AS A DECOY!
VERY CLEVER. BUT CAPTAIN BLACK HAS FALLEN FOR OUR DECOY. THIS TIME WE'LL GET HIM!
AT WESTON, THE TRUCK, SPOTTING THE INTERCEPTORS, SHOOTS OUT OF THE HANGAR...
THE ANGELS SWOOP DARINGLY LOW AS THE TRUCK SCREACHES DOWN THE RUNWAY...

MAKING IT TO THE GATE, THE TRUCK SWERVES VIOLENTLY, NARROWLY MISSING THE SPECTRUM SALOON CAR...
CAPTAIN SCARLET AND BLUE WASTE NO TIME...
HE'S MAKING FOR THE EAST ROAD.
AFTER HIM! ANGEL LEADER, DIVERT TRUCK AHEAD OF US!
S.I.G!
DESTINY ANGEL FIRES DIVERTING THE TRUCK BACK ONTO THE RUNWAY...
...AT THE END OF WHICH MAJOR GRAVENER HAS LANDED...
AS A HEAD-ON COLLISION SEEMS UNAVOIDABLE, THE TRUCK TWISTS CRAZILY OFF THE RUNWAY, CRASHING INTO AN OUTBUILDING...
IT'S NOT CAPTAIN BLACK!
THEN WHO?
HARRIS! IT'S HARRIS, MY DRIVER!
AT CLOUDBASE, SCARLET REFLECTS ON THE MYSTERONS INABILITY TO TELL THE REAL MAJOR FROM THEIR DUPLICATE...
WELL GENTLEMEN, IT SEEMS WE HAVE FOUND ANOTHER WEAKNESS.
YES SIR. LET'S HOPE WE CAN USE IT!

WORD SEARCH

Hidden in the wordsearch are some of Captain Scarlet™'s previous adventures.
Can you find them?

INFERNO
TRAITOR
MODEL SPV
THE TRAP
MANHUNT
AVALANCHE
OPERATION TIME
TREBLE CROSS
THE LAUNCHING
THE INQUISITION

A	I	P	R	R	O	S	L
V	N	P	O	T	P	S	A
A	Q	T	A	H	E	N	U
L	U	R	O	E	R	S	N
A	I	T	I	T	A	P	C
N	S	E	N	O	T	E	H
C	I	H	F	P	I	T	I
H	T	H	E	O	O	S	N
E	I	S	R	F	N	A	G
K	O	S	N	T	R	A	P
S	N	T	O	T	H	E	N
M	O	D	E	L	S	P	V
A	W	A	L	A	N	C	H
N	T	E	H	S	O	R	S
H	T	H	E	S	T	O	N
U	T	I	M	E	O	S	E
N	E	A	O	F	T	S	B
T	R	E	B	L	E	S	O
T	R	A	I	T	O	R	S

13. From what unique alloy is the SSC (Spectrum Saloon Car) made?

14. What is unusual about the driver's position in the SPV (Spectrum Pursuit Vehicle)?

15. What is the top speed of the Angel Interceptors?

RETURN TO BASE

You have crash landed on Mars and the Mysterons are after you.

To play this game you will need a dice and thin card.

Photocopy this page and then colour in your playing pieces :Captain Scarlet,™ Captain Blue ,Colonel White and Destiny Angel.

Stick your coloured copies on to card and then cut out your stand (Fig A) and slide together.

Now you are ready to play.

Throw the dice to decide who goes first and then move around the board...Beware though the Mysterons have traps:

Land on a Mysteron circle miss a go.

Land on an arrow go back three places.

Land on a Vortex and you gain another throw.

And if you land on a star you can use the short cut.

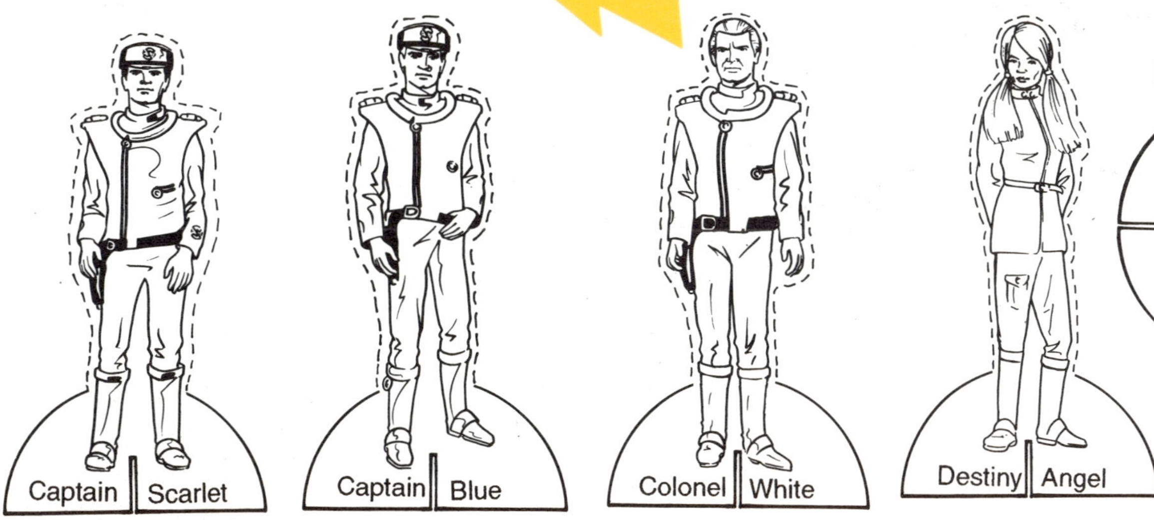

Fig A

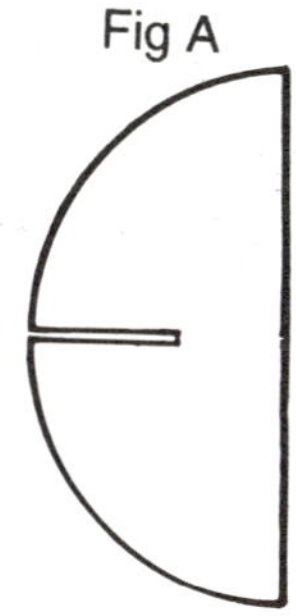

16. Which one of Spectrum's core team at Cloudbase comes from Australia?

17. Which essential function operates from the same deck of Cloudbase as the Generator Room?

18. The colours in the Spectrum badge run in bands from the centre, in the same order as the colours of the rainbow. Name them, in order, starting from the centre.

1
2
3
4
5
19
20
21
22
23
24
25
26
27
28
29
30
31
32
33
34
35
36

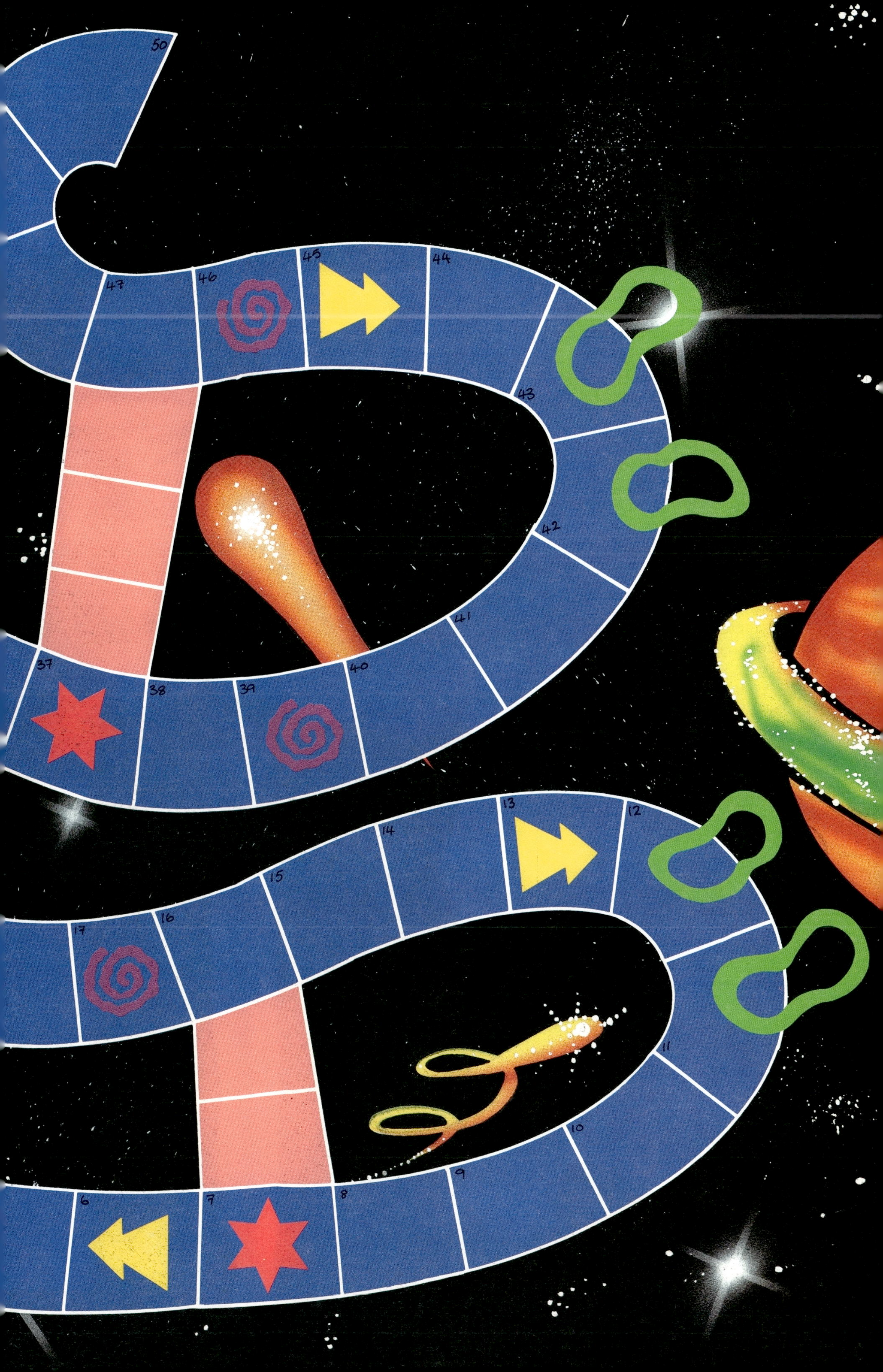

50
47
46
45
44
43
42
41
40
39
38
37
17
16
15
14
13
12
11
10
9
8
7
6

OPERATION TIME

The muted ticking of the wall clock was the only sound in the tense, sterile silence of the operating theatre. On the table in the centre of the room lay a motionless figure, completely covered except for a small, rectangular area across the forehead.

In the viewing booth above, two male nurses looked on.

"Will the patient be conscious throughout?" asked one.

"Yes", replied the other, "Dr. Magnus is using a local anaesthetic in order to monitor the patient's reactions."

In a strong, steady voice, the eminent brain surgeon urged the patient to relax. Applying the electrodes to the exposed forehead area and checking the pulse reading with his assisting colleague Dr. Turner, Magnus commanded:

"Switch on the cerebral pulsator."

As a high-pitched repeated bleep sounded, Dr. Magnus prepared to apply the electric current, well aware that one slip at this critical point could cost the patient his life, and him his career.

"OUR NEXT ACT OF RETALIATION WILL BE TO KILL TIME"

Wheeling round at his console to face the small audience of Spectrum Captains and Lieutenant Green, Colonel White was perplexed.

"What do they mean? Kill time?" he mused.

"The computer has compiled a list of everything related to time, Sir" volunteered Captain Scarlet.

"But it's over 14 micro files long", added Captain Blue, on a less positive note.

Aware that checking all these permutations would be a mammoth task, Colonel White realised they must narrow the field. After ordering a worldwide alert to all Spectrum Agents, he instructed his Captains to leave immediately for strategic cities across the globe: Blue to New York, Grey and Ochre to Rio De Janeiro and Moscow, Scarlet to London.

Later that evening, Doctors Magnus and Turner wished each other goodnight in the lobby of the capital's famous London Hospital.

"And how is the patient?" asked Magnus.

"Excellent. I expect a full recovery", replied Turner.

"Good", said Magnus, beaming "I was rather pleased myself."

"So we're all set for tomorrow?"

"Yes, I see no point in delaying. I'll go and see the

General straight away."

Leaving the hospital slumbering peacefully behind him, Magnus got into his car and swept out of the grounds, unaware of the eyes that followed him.

Seconds later, another car passed through the gates, its pale, black-clothed occupant steering the unmarked car in the direction Magnus had taken.

The journey from London Hospital to the prestigious Westbourne Clinic was a short one, and within fifteen minutes Dr. Magnus was reassuring his next patient.

"This release form I'd like you to sign is just a formality", he told the General, "But if you'd like a second opinion, we can delay the operation a week or so."

"No,no", the General replied in a heavily-accented voice,

"Let's get it over with tomorrow - give me the form and I'll sign it".

The General took up the pen and signed his name in a decisive hand: J.F.Tiempo.

Wishing his patient a good night's sleep, Dr.Magnus hurried back to his car, looking forward to getting some rest himself after the long stressful hours in the operating theatre.

The lights in his rearview mirror were at first merely irritating and then a little worrying. "He's far too close", thought Magnus, "Why doesn't he overtake?"

Drawing up at a red light, the Doctor was about to wave the car past when suddenly a shot rang out of the darkness and his windscreen shattered, sending glittering shards of glass cascading inwards. Realising that this was not simply an impatient driver but a serious threat, Magnus put his foot down and shot forward as the lights changed.

Heartbeat thudding loudly in his ears, he checked the mirror to see his pursuer's path blocked by another car at the crossroads.

"Lost him!" he muttered to himself.

Minutes later, the lights reappeared in a blinding flash, together with a harsh volley of shots from the car in pursuit, which was gaining on him at a seemingly superhuman rate. Driving now for his life, Magnus slammed down on the accelerator. But it was too late. The final shot had caught his rear tyre and the Doctor's car skidded wildly out of control, screaming off the road to somersault crazily down the rocky bank, finally exploding with a screaming and a deafening roar, and a billowing petrol-fed fireball thirty feet below.

Beside the shattered roadside fence, Mysteron Agent Captain Black's unnaturally pale face, lit eerily by the snaking flames, looked down without expression at the Doctor's broken body amid the wreckage. Turning, he addressed his new companion; an exact duplicate of the man he had just so ruthlessly sent to a hellish death. Black as the night itself, his deep, harsh voice commanded: "Doctor Magnus, tomorrow you will kill time...Tomorrow you will kill time."

As Destiny Angel swooped smoothly in to the landing platform, Spectrum's white-haired Commander In Chief paced Cloudbase's Control Room, frustrated by the lack of progress.

"Anything to report?" he barked, for the fifth time in as many minutes.

"No, Sir" replied Lieutenant Green with a sigh.

Suddenly, the loudspeakers came to life and Captain Magenta's highly excited voice brought both men to attention.

"I've got it Colonel! I've got it!"

Telling Magenta to calm down and start from the beginning, Colonel White listened as the Captain explained how the newspapers were reporting that General Tiempo, Commander of the Western Region Defence, was in London for an operation.

"Get to the point ,Captain!" rasped the Colonel, barely able to disguise his impatience.

"Well that's it, Sir! General Tiempo is a key target for the Mysterons. And Tiempo is Spanish for time. 'Kill time'. Kill Tiempo!"

As the man behind this revealing exchange slept peacefully at the Westbourne Clinic, the door to his room opened without a sound and a dark figure, equally soundless, approached the bed.

Without warning, light flooded the scene and Captain Scarlet's™ unmistakable voice questioned: "Doctor Magnus?"

Magnus wheeled round.

"Y-Yes. I...was just...checking on my patient. But who are you?"

As the General awoke, confused and blinking in the light, Scarlet replied: "Captain Scarlet, Spectrum World Security. I have orders to escort you both back to Cloudbase."

Safely ensconced at Cloudbase, General Tiempo listened gravely as Colonel White briskly outlined the Mysteron threat to his life and the need to keep watch over him round the clock because of it.

"Yes, but my patient was to undergo a serious brain operation tomorrow!" broke in Magnus furiously.

"We have the facilities here at Cloudbase for any operation," Captain Blue reassured him, "Don't you agree Doctor Fawn?"

"Yes", replied Spectrum's Chief Medical Officer quietly but firmly, "We have the facilities. But in view of the Mysteron threat, I suggest we postpone the operation for a week or so."

"Out of the question!" cried Magnus, "It must go ahead immediately!"

"But I understood..." protested Dr.Fawn.

"Immediately Doctor! IMMEDIATELY!!

"Alright" agreed Colonel White, after a tense pause, "He's your patient Doctor Magnus. Prepare the sick bay."

Early the next morning, Magnus impatiently instructed the radiographer taking X-rays of the General's head in various positions. Satisfied surprisingly quickly, he snapped: "That's enough. And get these to the theatre as soon as possible."

Minutes later, a preoccupied Colonel White, scanning the theatre on the internal TV screen, instructed Lieutenant Green: "Keep open contact with the sick bay. I want to hear every word that is said. I have a feeling that the Mysteron attempt on General Tiempo's life is very close."

As he took the X-rays down to the the theatre, the radiographer noticed the outline of a hand on one of the films.

"Hm! That Magnus should keep his hands to himself", he murmured, pleased to catch the Doctor out professionally, having been annoyed by his rude manner.

With proceedings underway, the air was even more full of tension than at the surgeon's last brain operation. Colonel White watched the screen intently as Magnus ordered:

"Switch on the cerebral pulsator. Set the voltage for 1.7."

"But that's far too high!" protested Dr. Fawn.

" I'm in charge here, Doctor", barked Magnus, applying the electrode to the patient's forehead.

Watching from the viewing booth above, the radiographer's eye was again caught by the General's X-rays, mounted on the light-wall. Unbelieving, he blinked, as if to question what his eyes told him. But no, there was no mistake; the hand he had noticed earlier had developed into a full positive image, starkly contrasting with the ghostly X-ray rendering of General Tiempo's skull.

"Impossible!" he breathed and rushed from the room with one thought only in his mind: to stop Magnus.

As the operation reached its critical point, Magnus, forehead beaded with sweat, seemed intent only on getting it over with. Dr. Turner watched in dismay as the patient's pulse and heart rates began to rise.

Pulse120...124...breathing irregular...deteriorating... "Magnus" he gasped.

Almost simultaneously, Colonel White's voice boomed out through the speakers: "Magnus is a Mysteron! Hold him!"

"It's too late", crowed Magnus viciously,"He's dead!"

"You're wrong", said Dr. Fawn, pulling back the sheet to reveal the patient,"You've killed Captain Scarlet™."

With lightning reaction, Magnus flung the instrument table at the stunned Dr. Turner and fled from the theatre, knocking over Captain Magenta - on guard outside the door - as he went.

As Lieutenant Green sounded the alert, Captain Blue found Captain Indigo along the corridor from the sick bay.

"He's locked himself in there", said Indigo, pointing at a door marked 'Generator Room', "But we can get in through the maintenance door."

"Good idea. But I'll go in alone", replied Blue, setting off in pursuit.

As he approached the Mysteron from behind, Captain Blue used all his powers of concentration to make no sound. But with an uncanny sixth sense, Magnus wheeled around, gun in hand.

"It's too late Magnus", said Blue steadily, "You've failed. Give yourself up now and we'll try to help you."

"You, help me?" sneered Magnus, "No, Earthman, even if I have failed, you shall die."

As he raised his gun, Blue grabbed for a nearby ladder and, using all his strength, flung it all at Magnus, thrusting him backwards and trapping him against the high voltage generator panel. Acrid smoke and sparks mingled with the shrieks of the foiled Mysteron shell of his body.

"I would like to thank Colonel White and everyone at Spectrum for their help", announced General Tiempo ceremoniously.

"And", added Colonel White, "Would like to thank Captain Scarlet for volunteering to take General Tiempo's place during the operation. Once again he saved the situation and demonstrated his remarkable powers of recovery." He went on to remind them of the two further discoveries they had made about the Mysterons - firstly, that they are impervious to X -rays and secondly that electricity is their Achilles heel.

"High voltage electric currents" he pronounced, "Can kill Mysterons as well as men."

19. How many miles above the surface of the ocean does Spectrum's HQ float?

20. What is Captain Scarlet that you are not?

ANSWERS

O J O W H I T E W E R T D C Y T
P O T N S C A R L D H M J Y R E R
E S T I N O M S C A H L E T U Y T R F G H
O A D R O F Y S C A L E T A O S E Y U H G R E S
T P B L U E P Y J G R E Y R C T R K I U U Y T R F
O K O T L O O M O E T P R S H I E N H T R E D E
L O O A P E R P T N R L O O R N D U Y T R N K J
H A R M O N Y H O T O E T D E Y O T R F D E W
P L E A S O F O K A G A E Y P E N H G R T R
O M E L O D Y N N O L S L O N H G T R
T O G R E E N Y S E O E K J H
E A T A W A S T R U B G F
R O S T A I N O M J U

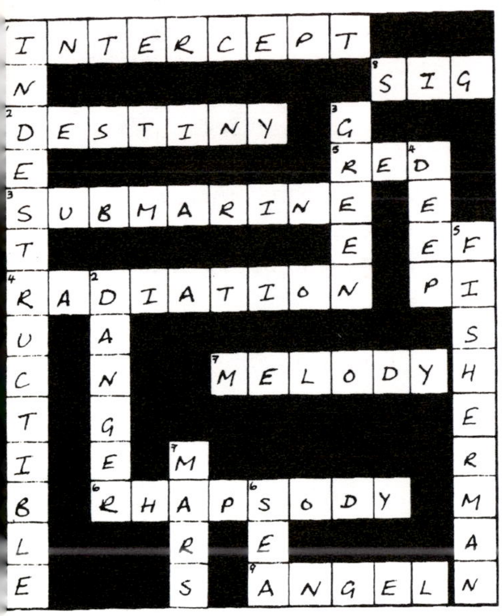

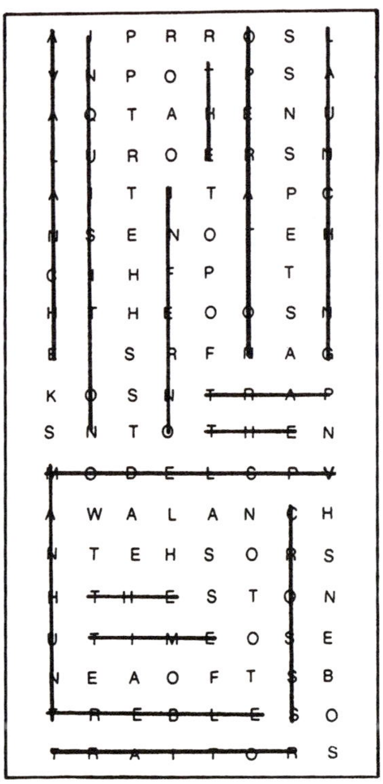

1. 600
2. Captain Black.
3. Deep sea diving and water sking.
4. By sensing their radiation field.
5. X-rays.
6. With electricity.
7. The Anti-Mysteron Electron Gun.
8. He was the youngest Colonel ever in the World Army Air Force.
9. His impetuous nature.
10. Futura City.
11. Compassion.
12. He feels pain, just like anyone else.
13. Fleetonium.
14. The driver faces backwards.
15. 3,000mph.
16. Dr. Fawn.
17. The sick bay, incorporating the operating theatre.
18. Red, orange, yellow, green, blue, indigo, violet.
19. 7 miles.
20. INDESTRUCTIBLE!